anythink

NATURAL SELECTION

JOYCE MCCORMICK

PowerKiDS press.

NEW YORK

Published in 2017 by The Rosen Publishing Group, Inc.
29 East 21st Street, New York, NY 10010

Editor: Melissa Raé Shofner
Book Design: Michael Flynn
Interior Layout: Reann Nye

Photo Credits: Cover Mike Hill/Photographer's Choice RF/Getty Images; p. 4 Rodrigo Friscione/Cultura/Getty Images; p. 5 Usagi-P/Shutterstock.com; p. 6 DEA/C. BEVILACQUA/De Agostini Picture Library/Getty Images; p. 7 (deer) Hein Nouwens/Shutterstock.com; p. 8 ET1972/Shutterstock.com; p. 9 yevgeniy11/Shutterstock.com; p. 11 (top) Stefano Bianchetti/Corbis Documentary/Getty Images; p. 11 (bottom) DnDavis/Shutterstock.com; p. 12 critterbiz/Shutterstock.com; p. 13 DEA PICTURE LIBRARY/Getty Images; p. 15 Mark Bridger/Shutterstock.com; p. 16 Steven Blandin/Shutterstock.com; p. 17 (large ground finch) Ralph Lee Hopkins/National Geographic/Getty Images; p. 17 (Grey Warbler Finch) Dethan Punalur/Stockbyte/Getty Images; p. 19 (top) Martin Fowler/Shutterstock.com; p. 19 (bottom) Steve McWilliam/Shutterstock.com; p. 20 Nagel Photography/Shutterstock.com; p. 21 Gerard Koudenburg/Shutterstock.com; p. 22 Albie Venter/Shutterstock.com.

Cataloging-in-Publication Data

Names: McCormick, Joyce.
Title: Natural selection / Joyce McCormick.
Description: New York : PowerKids Press, 2017. | Series: Spotlight on ecology and life science | Includes index.
Identifiers: ISBN 9781499425833 (pbk.) | ISBN 9781499425857 (library bound) | ISBN 9781499426120 (6 pack)
Subjects: LCSH: Darwin, Charles, 1809-1882--Juvenile literature.Natural selection--Juvenile literature.Genes--Juvenile literature.
Classification: LCC QH375.M33 2017 | DDC 576.8'2--dc23

Manufactured in China

CPSIA Compliance Information: Batch #BW17PK For further information contact Rosen Publishing, New York, New York at 1-800-237-9932.

CONTENTS

CHAPTER ONE

COMMON ANCESTRY

Think of all the different kinds of animals you know, from tiny one-inch-long (2.5 cm) bumblebee bats to 98-foot-long (30 m) blue whales. There are millions of different species, or kinds, of creatures on Earth. What's more, all of those millions of creatures are **descendants** of common **ancestors**!

Although they look different at first glance, human arms and whale fins actually have similar bone structure. The structure has evolved to suit the different needs of each species.

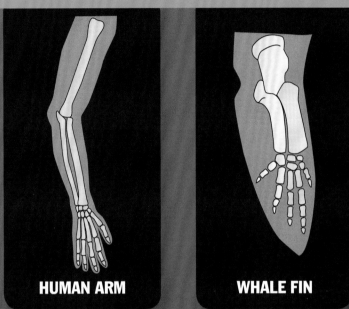

HUMAN ARM   **WHALE FIN**

Although all creatures are related to each other, common ancestry is more visible in animal groups, such as **mammals**, because members share an ancestor that lived more recently. For example, humans shared an ancestor with whales about 60 million years ago. Even though there are clear differences between the two species, we can still observe some similarities between them. But if all species are all related, how did they come to be so different?

Evolution is the process of living things changing over time. Natural selection is a process through which some of these changes occur.

CHAPTER TWO

HOW IT WORKS

Biologist Charles Darwin published his ideas about evolution by natural selection in his book *On the Origin of Species* in 1859. Darwin discussed the different kinds of selection that occur and the key parts of the process. The process of natural selection can be broken down into a few main steps: overpopulation, variation, competition, and selection.

Each generation of a species has more young than will probably survive. Each of these young has traits that set it apart from the others. Within each species, members have differences in how they look, sound, and behave. These differences are called variation.

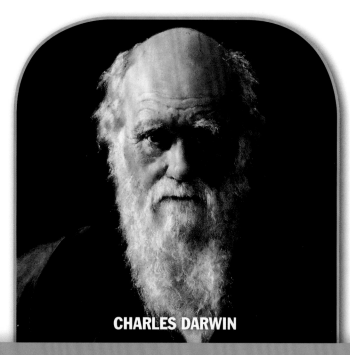

CHARLES DARWIN

Darwin is thought of as the father of evolution. His studies have changed the way people think about the history of Earth's species and where humans fit in.

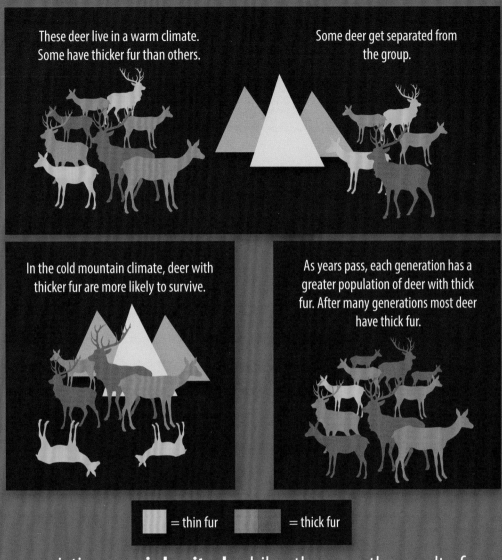

These deer live in a warm climate. Some have thicker fur than others.

Some deer get separated from the group.

In the cold mountain climate, deer with thicker fur are more likely to survive.

As years pass, each generation has a greater population of deer with thick fur. After many generations most deer have thick fur.

= thin fur   = thick fur

Some variations are **inherited**, while others are the result of conditions in an organism's **environment**.

There are more animals living on Earth than can be supported by its **resources**. Animals compete for food, shelter, and breeding partners. Members that successfully survive set the trend for the evolution of the species.

CHAPTER THREE

MUTATIONS

DNA is a chemical that contains code. This code tells an organism's cells what to do. Mutations occur when DNA is **damaged** or changed. Sometimes this changed DNA doesn't have any effect on an organism. Sometimes it has a small or large effect.

Mutations can be common within species, but their type and location are **random**. When mutations occur, natural selection decides if they will continue. Some mutations will give an organism a better chance at surviving, reproducing, and passing on this mutation. These mutations may continue within the species. Other mutations will mean an organism has a harder time surviving and reproducing. These organisms and their mutations may die out. This natural selection is one of the ways that evolution happens. Helpful mutations may become a normal part of the species.

MUTATED APPLE

Mutations within this turtle's DNA caused it to have two heads. Do you think this mutation will be helpful or harmful?

CHAPTER FOUR

PASS IT ON

Genes are made of DNA. Genes affect how an organism will look and behave. For example, a person whose parents have curly hair is also likely to have curly hair. The gene for curly hair is passed from parents to their offspring, or young. Evolution takes place when a species' genes change over time and are passed down through each generation.

Humans haven't always looked the way they do today. Over time, our bodies have evolved. A modern human's jaw and teeth are smaller than those of earlier humans. As humans developed, or grew, larger brains, the shape of their skull and forehead also changed. These physical, or bodily, changes didn't happen all at once, but over many generations. The physical changes in human species are the result of certain genes, such as the genes for a smaller jaw, being passed down from parent to offspring.

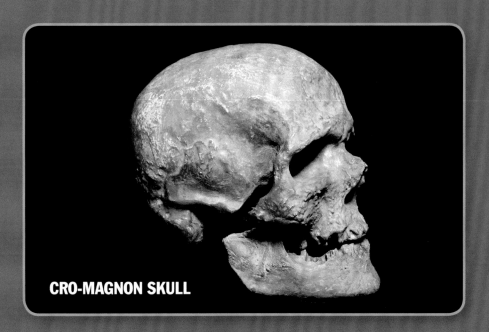

CRO-MAGNON SKULL

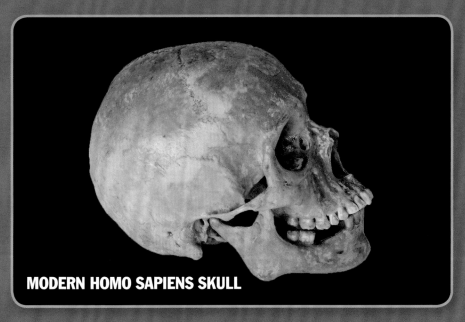

MODERN HOMO SAPIENS SKULL

Fossils show us proof of the evolutionary changes that species undergo over time. Evolutionary biologists, scientists who study the evolution of living organisms, may try to figure out what a species might look like in the future.

CHAPTER FIVE

SURVIVAL OF THE FITTEST

The goal of every living creature is to survive and create offspring. Animals that have certain beneficial genetic **traits** are more likely to accomplish this goal than others. A quality that improves an organism's chance of survival is called a favorable trait.

Predator and prey relationships are a key part of natural selection. Animals will pass on the genes that make them better hunters. Prey animals that are better at avoiding predators will also pass on their favorable genes.

For a giraffe, having a long neck is a favorable trait. A longer neck gives a giraffe the advantage of being able to reach higher into trees for more leaves to eat. Since it's better fed, this giraffe will likely be stronger and faster than those that must work harder to compete for food. The long-necked giraffe will create offspring that carry the gene for this favorable trait into future generations.

Animals that are better **adapted** for survival will pass on their traits to the next generation of their species. In this way, natural selection affects which genes continue to be passed on, and thus how a species will evolve.

CHAPTER SIX

TYPES OF SELECTION

Variations of a trait can be observed across a species. For example, most sunflowers may be medium height, but some may be very tall and some may be short. There is a range of sizes, with most of the population somewhere around an average between the two **extremes**.

Stabilizing selection occurs when pressures keep the trend toward the average. If the short plants can't reach enough sunlight and the tall plants are damaged by wind, neither group will be able to survive and reproduce as well. The medium plants will survive to pass on their height trait.

Directional selection pushes the trend toward one of the extremes. If an organism has a favorable extreme trait that gives it an advantage, the trait is likely to be passed on. Disruptive selection occurs when the average population suffers, which makes traits at both extremes more likely to occur.

Traits, such as coat color, vary within a species. If one color helps the animals of a species blend in with their surroundings and avoid predators, it's considered a favorable trait that's likely to be passed on through directional selection.

CHAPTER SEVEN

DARWIN'S FINCHES

Every species is part of an ecosystem, which is a community of living things and the nonliving parts of their environment. Within an ecosystem, each species has a niche, or a function that it fills there. A niche involves what the species contributes to its ecosystem and how it affects the ecosystem as it eats, makes its home, and reproduces.

Darwin formed his ideas about evolution by natural selection when studying finches from the Galapagos Islands. He discovered that, from a common finch species, several other species of finches had evolved to fill their own ecological niches. The finches had evolved different beaks that were adapted to the type of food they ate. Their beaks were shaped to help them eat insects, seeds, or nectar. Although the birds shared similar habits and bodies, they had evolved to be better adapted to their particular home and way of life.

MEDIUM GROUND FINCH

LARGE
GROUND FINCH

GREY WARBLER FINCH

At least 13 species of Galapagos finches evolved from one original species.

CHAPTER EIGHT

HUMAN INFLUENCE

Over the past few hundred years, the human population has grown a lot. People have harmed the environment by building cities and roads and by overusing resources. Human activities have even affected natural selection.

The **Industrial Revolution** shaped the evolution of the peppered moth. Peppered moths are native to Europe. Their coloring can vary, but before the Industrial Revolution most moths living near London, England, tended to be white with black markings. A rare gene caused some moths to be black. White speckled moths used their coloring for camouflage, or to blend in with their surroundings. Against a tree trunk, a white peppered moth could barely be seen.

During the Industrial Revolution, dark smoke and ash from factories made it easier for dark moths to hide from predators. The white speckled moths began to drop in number. In this way, human activities caused a rare genetic trait to become more common.

Which of the three types of natural selection does the case of the peppered moth exhibit?

CHAPTER NINE

ARTIFICIAL SELECTION

People have directly shaped the evolution of certain species by practicing artificial selection. Artificial selection is the process of purposely causing favorable traits to be reproduced in plants and animals.

The food in grocery stores has changed over time. Corn, for example, has become bigger and juicier through

GRAY WOLF

All domesticated, or tame, dogs are descended from gray wolves. Domesticated dogs are the result of artificial selection. Specialized dog breeds were developed by breeding animals with favorable traits.

artificial selection. Artificial selection is also used to breed larger livestock, such as cows and chickens.

People argue about whether artificial selection is a good idea. When selection occurs in nature, favorable traits change a species' evolutionary trend but there's still variety. It's important for variety to be present because traits that are favorable at one time may not be at another. Variety allows shifts to occur as needed. Artificial selection reduces variety by making all members of a population very similar. This may put a species at risk.

CHAPTER TEN

WHAT'S NEXT?

Natural selection is constantly occurring. Earth's species have undergone amazing changes over time and will continue to evolve. What does the future hold for life on Earth?

Human activities have lead to global climate change, causing temperatures near Earth's surface to rise. Higher temperatures change weather conditions, affecting the way ecosystems function. Some members of a species may have traits that allow them to survive and pass those traits down through natural selection. If not, the species may go extinct, or die out.

Just as variety within a species is important to its survival, having a variety of many species on Earth is necessary to the health of the planet. Like every other living species, humans evolved from a common ancestor to become what we are today. How can we use the advancements we've made to help and defend our plant and animal relatives?

GLOSSARY

adapt (uh-DAPT) To change in order to live better in a certain environment.

ancestor (AN-ses-tuhr) An animal that lived before others in its family tree.

damage (DAA-mij) To cause harm.

descendant (dih-SEN-duhnt) An animal that comes from an animal of an earlier time.

environment (en-VY-ruhn-muhnt) The conditions that surround a living thing and affect the way it lives.

extreme (ik-STREEM) Going past the expected or common. Extreme weather might be very hot or very cold.

genes (JEENZ) Many tiny parts in the center of a cell. Genes tell your cells how your body will look and act.

Industrial Revolution (in-DUS-tree-ul reh-vuh-LOO-shun) A time in history beginning in the mid-1700s, when power-driven machines were first used to produce goods in large quantities, changing the way people lived and worked.

inherit (in-HEHR-it) To receive something from a parent.

mammal (MAA-mul) Any warm-blooded animal whose babies drink milk and whose body is covered with hair or fur.

random (RAAN-duhm) Lacking or seeming to lack a regular plan, purpose, or pattern.

resource (REE-sors) Something that can be used.

trait (TRAYT) A feature or characteristic.

INDEX

PRIMARY SOURCE LIST

Page 6
Portrait of Charles Robert Darwin. Oil on canvas. Painting by John Collier. 1881. Now kept at the National Portrait Gallery, London, England.

Page 11
(Top) Fossilized Cro-Magnon skull. Now held at the Upper Paleolithic Natural History Museum, Milan, Italy.

Page 19
(Top) White peppered moth. Photograph by Martin Fowler. From Shutterstock.com.
(Bottom) Melanic peppered moth. Photograph by Steve McWilliam. From Shutterstock.com.

WEBSITES

Due to the changing nature of Internet links, PowerKids Press has developed an online list of websites related to the subject of this book. This site is updated regularly. Please use this link to access the list: www.powerkidslinks.com/sels/natsel